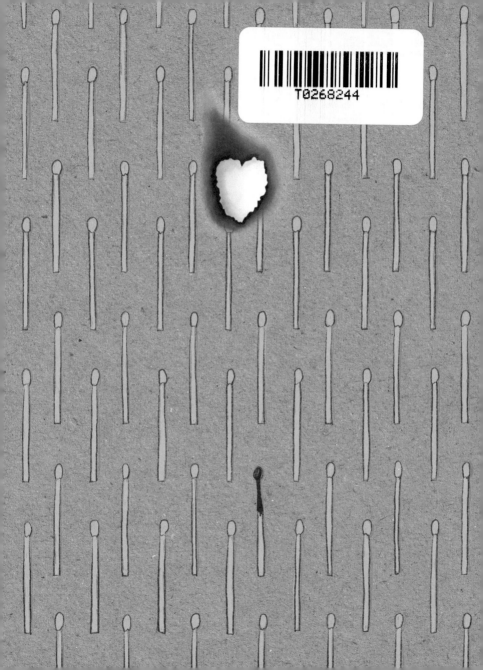

A LITTLE BOOK ABOUT FIRE

This book is for all the people with the fire inside
(you know who you are)

Thank you ♡ to

My ever patient and beating-me-at-heardle husband, Sean
for the unwavering belief, ping-pong, and coffee.

The creative people who see my spark even when I can't
and answer my messages the most:
Maureen, Jenee, Robin, Rodney, and Evan.

My publishers Susan, and Lauren, designers Doug and Steve for
being so very skilled at what they do.

Mr Blue (who insisted on being in the book somewhere) for always
being a good boy

Those I left in England and miss every day, Jon, Ian,
Hollie, Jamie, Joe, Bennett, Mark, Mila and Bella.

Those who read dedication pages (you are my people).

A LITTLE BOOK ABOUT FIRE
(and the people that have it inside them)

written & illustrated by

Aileen Bennett

Some people have a little fire somewhere inside
It doesn't show up on X-rays,

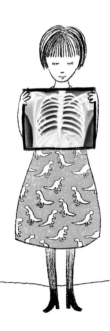

(Except when it can)

It fuels a drive, an energy,
A tendency to shine,

Even beneath an overcoat

Or hiding at the back of a room

Sometimes it rains

It drizzles for days

It pours

And yet, the fire is still there

Every so often, it gets out of hand
Overwhelming everything

Is that how forest fires start?

Sometimes the flame hides,
staying teeny tiny for years,

No more than a barely-glowing ember
That hasn't given up but doesn't offer warmth

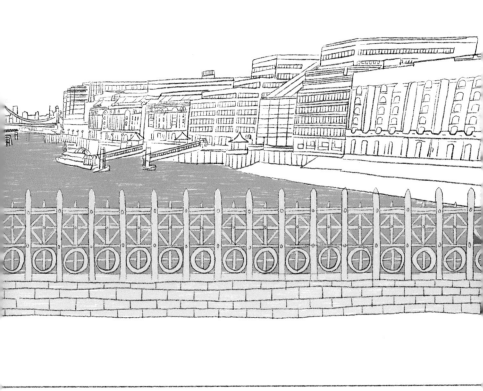

It's taken for granted and ignored
While the people with the fire inside
Find comfort in safer things that don't burn

One day, they question where their fire went

Forgetting that it burns brightest
when its fed knowledge

And love
And fun
And tries new things

Especially new things
(And old things that are new)

The embers glow, hidden from the world
The embers grow, hidden from the person

Then just at the right time
The flame explodes into life

(sometimes it explodes slowly)

And the best bit is
Remembering who they were
Remembering who they are

The people who have this little flame
Often recognize others
with this heat burning inside

They can see the fire in other people because
They can feel it in themselves

When they fan the flames of their own fire

The sparks start little fires inside others.

Aileen Bennett is an illustrator, writer, speaker, and creative director. She is originally from Essex, England, and has lived in the United States for nearly twenty years.

Happily married to an American, when she isn't traveling, she works from a white studio with the assistance of a white dog called Mr Blue.

She has an insatiable curiosity, bulletproof enthusiasm, and a slight obsession with surfing.

You can find her illustrations, thoughts and other things on instagram @aileensnotebook

This little book was written as Aileen was completing chemotheraphy treatment and was wondering if she'd get her spark back. (She did)

SUSAN SCHADT PRESS
www.susanschadtpress.com

Published in 2023 by Susan Schadt Press, L.L.C.
New Orleans

Copyright ©2023 Aileen Bennett

All rights reserved. No part of this publication may be reproduced, stored in a retrival system, or transmitted in any form or by any means, electronic, mechanical, photocopying or otherwise without prior permission in writing from the publisher.

Design by Doug Turshen | Steve Turner

Library of Congress Control Number: 2023908247
ISBN: 979-8-9874780-1-1
Printed in China by WKT Company Limited

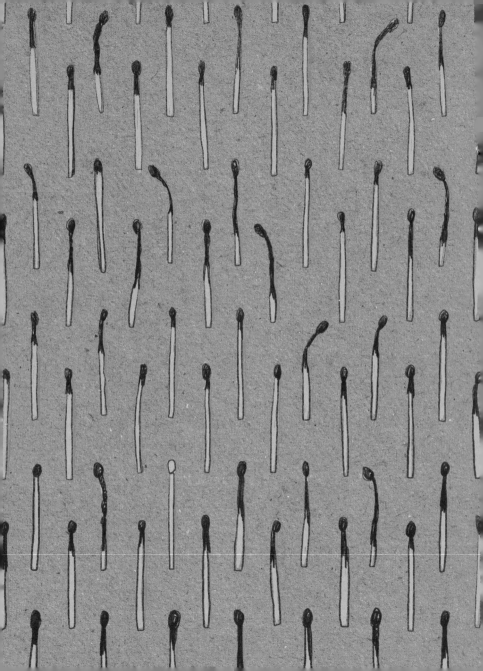